Roti Revival

OrangeBooks Publication

1st Floor, Rajhans Arcade, Mall Road, Kohka, Bhilai, Chhattisgarh 490020

Website:**www.orangebooks.in**

© Copyright, 2024, Author

All rights reserved. No part of this book may be reproduced, stored in a retrieval system, or transmitted, in any form by any means, electronic, mechanical, magnetic, optical, chemical, manual, photocopying, recording or otherwise, without the prior written consent of its writer.

First Edition, 2024

ISBN: 978-93-6554-536-4

ARUSHI CHATTERJEE'S Cook Book

ROTI Revival

A TEEN'S GUIDE FOR A GLUTEN-FREE LIFE

Featured in

THE TIMES OF INDIA

OrangeBooks Publication
www.orangebooks.in

Dedication

To my amazing friends (you know who you are) - thank you for being my forever taste testers and for your rather honest reviews. Your enthusiasm fuels my love for cooking, and I can't wait to share these recipes with you again and again.

Introduction

Welcome to my recipe book! My gluten-free cooking journey began in Italy, where I fell in love with pizza and pasta, only to discover I had a gluten intolerance after returning to India. The pandemic turned me into a passionate cook, adapting my favorite dishes to be gluten-free. Though my intolerance has faded, I still love gluten-free meals for their inclusivity and flavor. This book is a collection of my labor of love, filled with recipes tested and approved by family, friends, and those with celiac disease. I hope you enjoy making these dishes as much as I do!

Gluten-Free Recipes

Breakfast

Waffles 3
Pancakes 6

Appetizers

Quesadillas 10
Vietnamese Potato Pancakes 13
Bruschetta 16
Vietnamese Spring Rolls 19
Pesto Pasta 22

Mains

Pasta in Marinara Sauce 26
Chicken & Mushroom Alfredo Sauce Pasta 30
Mushroom Wontons with Thai Curry Soup 34
Garlic-Butter Shrimp 38
Egg Fried Rice 41
Shrimp Tacos 44
Caramelized Onion Pasta 47

Desserts

Chocolate Cupcakes 51
Rice Cake Delights 55
Brownies 58
Blondies 62

Waffles

Ingredients:

1. 2 cups almond flour
2. 1 tbsp powdered sugar **(Optional)**
3. 1 tbsp baking powder
4. 1/4 tsp salt
5. 1 3/4 cups buttermilk
6. 2 large eggs
7. 2 tsp vanilla extract
8. 1/2 cup melted unsalted butter + more for greasing the waffle iron

Method:

- Melt the unsalted butter in the microwave and let it cool to room temperature.
- Start preheating your waffle iron. This takes about 5-10 mins, which is about the same amount of time it takes for your waffle batter to come together.
- Add the almond flour, powdered sugar, baking powder, and salt to a larger mixing bowl and whisk them together.
- To the dry ingredients, add the eggs, vanilla extract, melted unsalted butter, and half of the buttermilk and mix.
- While mixing, gradually add the remaining buttermilk.

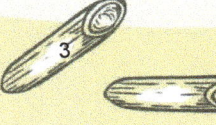

- Check the consistency of the waffle batter - it should be smooth and a little thick. Ensure there are no lumps in the batter.
- You can add more buttermilk to adjust the consistency of the batter to your liking.
- Grease the preheated waffle iron with melted unsalted butter or cooking spray.
- Add about ½ a cup of batter into the iron, and close immediately to start the cooking process.
- The waffles take about 10 minutes to cook.
- After the waffles are ready (they should be crisp and have a golden brown color when they are ready) take them out of the waffle iron and serve on a plate.
- Top with whipped cream, fresh fruit, maple syrup, chocolate syrup (or any of your other favorite toppings) and enjoy!

Top Tips:

- Preheating the waffle iron makes the process of cooking waffles faster.
- You can substitute almond flour with an all-purpose gluten-free flour blend.
- Ensure the eggs and melted butter are at room temperature before adding them to the waffle batter.
- This recipe makes quite a few waffles, which are easy to store in the freezer, so you can make them ahead of time, and warm them up when you are ready to eat.
- Ensure you only use unsalted butter; using salted butter will make the waffles overly savoury.
- You can skip adding powdered sugar to the waffle batter if you prefer to add your sweeteners as toppings, or for any dietary restrictions.

Pancakes

Ingredients:

1. 1½ cups of gluten-free all purpose flour
2. 4 tsp baking powder
3. ¼ tsp salt
4. 2 tbsp sugar **(Optional)**
5. 1 large egg
6. 1¼ cups milk
7. ¼ cup melted butter unsalted butter + more for cooking
8. 1 tsp vanilla essence

Method:

- ▲ Whisk together the dry ingredients i.e. the gluten-free all-purpose flour, baking powder, salt, and sugar in a large mixing bowl.
- ▲ Crack the egg in the bowl with the dry ingredients, add the unsalted butter, vanilla essence, and half of the milk and mix well.
- ▲ Whilst mixing, add in the remainder of the milk.
- ▲ The batter for the pancakes should not be runny, it should be thick enough to scoop.
- ▲ You can adjust the quantity of the milk depending on your batter consistency preferences.
- ▲ Heat a flat-top pan, and add some unsalted butter/olive oil to grease the pan.

- ▲ To the hot pan, add a scoop of pancake batter and cook on low-medium flame.

- ▲ Flip the pancake in about 2-3 minutes, and cook the other side for about the same amount of time.

- ▲ The pancake is ready when there is a golden brown color on both sides.

- ▲ Repeat the cooking process for the rest of the batter.

- ▲ Serve the pancakes hot with maple syrup, whipped cream, fresh berries, or any other toppings of your liking.

Top Tips:

- ▲ 4 teaspoons of baking powder may seem like a lot, but this is the key to making the pancakes perfectly fluffy.

- ▲ Ensure the egg and melted unsalted butter are at room temperature before adding them to the batter.

- ▲ You can use your favorite non-dairy milk, such as almond milk, if you prefer lighter pancakes.

- ▲ This pancake batter makes quite a few pancakes, so serve it for family and friends, or make them ahead of time and freeze to enjoy later.

Quesadillas

Ingredients:

1. 1 cup of diced mushrooms
1. ½ of an onion, diced
2. 4 large garlic cloves, minced
3. ½ cup of sweet corn, boiled
4. ¼ cup of tomatoes, diced
5. Corn tortillas
6. Shredded mozzarella cheese
7. Lemon
8. Salt
9. Pepper
10. Chili oil
11. Olive oil

Method:

- On a hot pan, add olive oil and cook the diced onion on medium-high heat for 5 minutes.
- Then add the garlic, and cook on medium-low heat for about 1 minute.
- Just as the garlic turns golden in color, add the diced mushrooms, tomatoes and corn and sauté for about 7-10 minutes, till the mushrooms shrink down to half their size.
- Season with salt, pepper and chili oil to taste.

- ▲ Add the juice of half a lemon, and mix.
- ▲ Your filling is now ready; taste and adjust the seasoning as per your preferences.
- ▲ In another hot flat-top pan, add some olive oil.
- ▲ Once the oil is hot, place a corn tortilla on the pan, and reduce the heat to low.
- ▲ To assemble the quesadilla, on half of the tortilla, place 4-5 tablespoons of the filling and top with the shredded cheese.
- ▲ Fold the other half (without filling on it) in a way that it lands on top of the half with filling on it.
- ▲ Cook till the bottom of the quesadilla turns golden brown.
- ▲ Slide the quesadilla onto a plate, cut in half and serve hot!

Top Tips:

- ▲ You can substitute the chili oil for your favorite hot sauce.
- ▲ Ensure you shred your own cheese, rather than buying pre-shredded cheese, it makes all the difference.
- ▲ You can add almost any vegetable to this quesadilla - mushrooms, corn and tomatoes are what I like best. This makes this recipe a great way to use up vegetables that have been sitting in your fridge for a while.
- ▲ When assembling the quesadilla ensure the heat is on the lowest setting, so that the corn tortilla does not burn. With some practice you will be able to assemble quesadillas quickly, ensuring that the tortilla does not burn.
- ▲ This recipe is vegetarian and not necessarily authentic, but everyone loves it!

Vietnamese Potato Pancakes

Ingredients:
1. 2 large potatoes
2. Ice cubes
3. Cornstarch
4. Salt
5. Pepper
6. Green onions (Also Known as Spring Onions/Scallions)
7. Chili Oil
8. Olive oil

Method:
- Finely chop the green onions & separate the whites and the greens.
- Shred the 2 large potatoes and squeeze out the retained water.
- Make an ice bath, with a lot of ice and water, and put the shredded potatoes in the ice water. (this will draw out the starch)
- Let the potatoes sit in the ice-water bath for about 10 minutes.

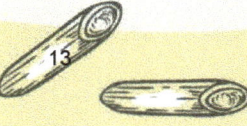

- Then squeeze all the water out and transfer the dry shredded potatoes to a large bowl.
- Season the dry potatoes with salt and pepper to taste.
- Add 2 tablespoons of cornstarch to the potatoes and mix.
- Add the white part of the green onion to the potato mixture and mix.
- Heat a pan, grease with olive oil and transfer the potato mixture to the pan, ensure there's an even layer of potatoes on the pan, and that the layer is about ¼ of an inch thick. You can make smaller pancakes or cover the entire surface area of the pan to make larger (more traditional) pancakes.
- Cook on medium-low flame for about 5 minutes, till there is a golden brown crust formed.
- Flip the pancake and cook for another 4-5 minutes.
- Transfer to a plate, and dab off the excess oil using paper tissue.
- Serve with the green part of the chopped green onions and a drizzle of chili oil.

Top Tips:

- Use a plate to help you flip the potato pancake if you are worried about breaking it.
- Season generously with salt and pepper because otherwise, you may risk your potato pancake being bland.

Bruschetta

Ingredients:
1. Gluten-free sourdough bread
2. Olive oil
3. 3 tomatoes, diced
4. ½ an onion, diced
5. 4 garlic cloves, minced
6. Salt
7. Oregano
8. Chili Oil

Method:
- Grease a heated pan with olive oil.
- Once the oil is hot add the chopped onions and sauté for about 5 minutes on medium-low heat.
- As soon as the onions turn translucent, add the minced garlic and sauté for another minute.
- Then, add the diced tomatoes, and salt to taste and sauté.
- Cook the tomatoes for about 6-7 minutes, till they turn soft but not mushy.
- Season the tomato mixture with 1 tablespoon of oregano.
- Grease another heated pan with olive oil.

- ▲ Place a slice of gluten-free sourdough bread and toast on low heat for about 3 minutes, When the bottom turns golden brown, flip the slice of bread and toast the other side for 3 more minutes.

- ▲ Place the golden brown slice of bread on a plate, add the tomato mixture on top, drizzle with chili oil and serve.

Top Tips:

- ▲ You can use any type of gluten-free bread, but sourdough works best.

- ▲ Ensure you taste the tomato mixture and adjust the seasoning to your liking.

- ▲ The chili oil is optional, but highly recommended.

- ▲ If you would like to serve a prettier appetizer, you can chop the green part of some green onions and sprinkle that on top of the bruschetta.

- ▲ This recipe is not necessarily authentic, but it is delicious!

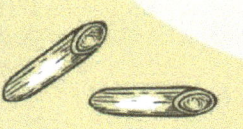  

Vietnamese Spring Rolls

Ingredients:

1. Rice paper
2. Julienned carrots
3. Julienned cucumbers
4. Lettuce leaves
5. Peeled and deveined shrimp
6. Salt
7. Peanut butter
8. Soy sauce
9. Fish sauce
10. Maple syrup

Method:

- To poach the shrimp, boil it in water, add salt, and place the shrimp in it for 4-5 minutes. Once the shrimp turns an orange-pink color, take them out.

- Wet a sheet of rice paper, and in the center, place a few pieces of shrimp first, then on top place a few pieces of carrots and cucumbers, and then finally a rolled-up lettuce leaf.

- Then roll the rice paper to form your spring roll.

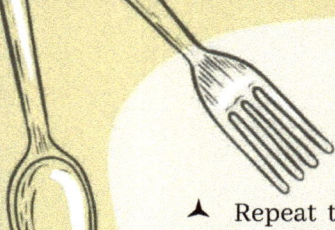

- Repeat this process till you have as many spring rolls as you would like.
- For the dipping sauce, in a bowl add a tbsp of peanut butter, 1 tsp of soy sauce, 1 tsp of fish sauce, 1 tsp of maple syrup, and salt to taste, and whisk till it comes together.
- Enjoy the spring rolls with the dipping sauce.

Top Tips:

- You can use any vegetables lying around; carrots and cucumbers work well.
- You can use any protein, like chicken. Shrimp is just easier to cook. Or you could skip the shrimp and keep it vegetarian.
- Ensure you don't over-fill the spring roll, that is key.
- The first few rolls can look a little flimsy, but they will become perfect with practice.
- The secret is the dipping sauce; you can adjust it to your liking but try not to skip it.

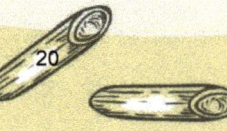

Pesto Pasta

Ingredients:
1. Fresh basil leaves (1 cup)
2. Pine nuts (⅓ cup)
3. Cashews (optional)
4. Peeled large garlic cloves (2-3)
5. Parmesan cheese (not the pre-shredded one, an actual block, ⅔ cups)
6. Extra virgin olive oil (½ cup + more for later)
7. 4 ice cubes
8. Salt
9. Rice pasta/lentil pasta

Method:
- In a blender/food processor blend together the basil, pine nuts, cashews (optional), garlic cloves, parmesan cheese, and 4 ice cubes, with only ⅓ of the olive oil first.
- Then open the lid, stir the contents around, add the remaining olive oil and blend again.
- You can add more olive oil after this, to get the pesto to your desired consistency.
- Add a teaspoon of salt and blend for the last time.

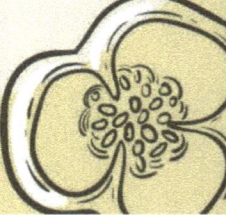

- ▲ Add the pesto to boiled rice-pasta/lentil-pasta, along with a little bit of the pasta water, and mix.
- ▲ Add some more parmesan cheese on top and serve!

Top Tips:

- ▲ Keep adding olive oil so that the pesto emulsifies.
- ▲ Add 4 ice cubes - this enhances the bright green color.
- ▲ Add cashews along with pine nuts, if you prefer a creamy pesto.
- ▲ Ensure that you salt the pasta water well.
- ▲ Use the best quality extra virgin olive oil available; it makes all the difference.
- ▲ This recipe makes enough pesto for 4 servings

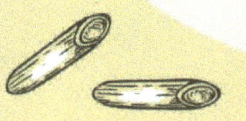

Pasta in Marinara Sauce

Ingredients:
1. Extra virgin olive oil
2. ½ of an onion, diced
3. 4 garlic cloves, minced
4. 3 tomatoes, diced
5. Salt
6. Hot sauce (optional)
7. Lemon
8. Rice pasta/Lentil pasta
9. Parmesan cheese (optional)

Method:
- In a pot, boil water and add a generous amount of salt.
- Add the rice/lentil pasta to the pot and let it cook as per package instructions.
- Whilst the pasta cooks, on a separate pan, heat some olive oil.
- To the pan add the diced onions and sauté on medium-low heat for 5 minutes, or until translucent.
- Then add the minced garlic and sauté for another minute.
- As the garlic turns golden brown, add the diced tomatoes and sauté.

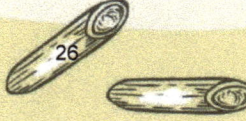

- ▲ Add some pasta water (starchy water that the pasta is boiling in) to the tomatoes and sprinkle in some salt.
- ▲ Cook the tomatoes for about 7 minutes till they become mushy.
- ▲ Turn off the heat and let the tomato mixture cool down for a few minutes.
- ▲ Transfer the tomato mixture to a blender jar, and add 2 ice cubes.
- ▲ Then blend till a sauce is formed.
- ▲ Add the sauce back to the pan, and turn on the heat to the lowest setting.
- ▲ To the tomato sauce, add 1 tsp of oregano and salt to taste.
- ▲ Add ½ a ladle of pasta water and cook the sauce for about 2 minutes.
- ▲ Then add a drizzle of hot sauce to the above (optional) and mix.
- ▲ Add the boiled pasta to the pan and mix until well combined.
- ▲ Add the juice of half a lemon and mix.
- ▲ Taste, and adjust the seasoning.
- ▲ Serve hot with grated parmesan cheese on top.

Top Tips:

- ▲ Ensure that you salt the pasta water well.
- ▲ Use the best quality extra virgin olive oil available, it makes all the difference.

▲ The cheese and hot sauce are optional, but highly recommended.

▲ This is not the authentic marinara sauce that you would get in Italy, but it is rather delicious, and it is easy to make, with ingredients that you probably already have lying around at home.

▲ This recipe is a crowd-pleaser, and re-heats well.

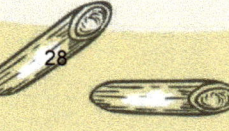

Chicken & Mushroom Alfredo Sauce Pasta

Ingredients:

1. 250 grams of chicken thigh, cut into small bite-sized pieces
2. Extra virgin olive oil
3. Butter
4. Red chili powder
5. Salt
6. Pepper
7. Chili Oil
8. Lemon
9. 400 grams of mushrooms, sliced
10. ½ of an onion, diced
11. 4 garlic cloves, minced
12. Milk
13. Cream
14. Oregano
15. Rice pasta/Lentil pasta
16. Any kind of processed cheese

Method:

- To marinate the chicken - add 2 tbsps of olive oil, ½ tsp of red chili powder, salt & pepper to taste, 1 tsp of chili oil, and the juice of half a lemon.
- Let the chicken marinate for at least 30 minutes before cooking.
- Grease a hot pan with olive oil.
- Cook the chicken on high heat for 7 minutes on each side.
- Once cooked, take the chicken out of the pan and set it aside.
- In the same pan, add a knob of butter and as the butter melts, add in the onions.
- Sauté the onions on medium-low heat for about 5 minutes or until translucent.
- As the onions turn translucent, add the minced garlic, and sauté for another minute.
- As soon as the garlic turns golden brown, add the mushrooms and sprinkle in some salt. Sauté the mushrooms for about 10 minutes, to cook them down. The size of the mushrooms should decrease significantly.
- As the mushrooms are cooking, in a separate pot, boil water, add salt to the water, and put in your rice/lentil pasta. Cook the pasta as per package instructions.
- After the mushrooms have been cooked, add 100 ml of milk and 100 ml of cream, and stir until the sauce comes to a simmer.
- Add the chopped chicken that had been set aside earlier.
- Season with salt, pepper and oregano to taste.

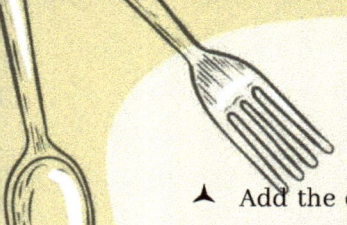

- Add the cheese along with some pasta water and mix until the cheese melts into the sauce.

- The alfredo sauce is now ready, add in the boiled pasta and mix.

- Turn off the heat, to ensure that the sauce remains creamy and does not become too thick. Then, taste and adjust the seasoning. Serve this dish hot!

Top Tips:

- Ensure that you salt the pasta water well.

- You can skip the chicken, to make this recipe vegetarian.

- If you are using chicken, try using chicken thighs instead of chicken breast to avoid dry pieces of chicken.

- Use a 1:1 ratio of milk to cream.

- Undercook your pasta, by boiling it for 2-3 minutes less than what the package instructions say. This is because the pasta will finish cooking in the sauce.

- This recipe is a little time-consuming, but the end result is a restaurant-quality dish that is worth all the hard work.

Mushroom Wontons with Thai Curry Soup

Ingredients:

1. Olive oil
2. 1 onion, diced
3. 6 cloves of garlic, minced
4. 1 cup of mushrooms, diced finely
5. 1 cup of cabbage, shredded
6. Salt
7. Pepper
8. Soy sauce
9. 2 cups of gluten-free all-purpose flour
10. Red thai curry paste
11. 2 cups of coconut milk
12. 1 cup of vegetable stalk
13. Fish sauce
14. Lemon
15. Chili Oil

Method:

- ▲ To make the dough for the dumplings, in a large mixing bowl slowly add water to 2 cups of gluten-free all-purpose flour, and sprinkle in some salt to taste. Knead until a dough is formed.
- ▲ Let the dough rest for at least 30 minutes.
- ▲ While the dough rests, start working on the filling for the wontons.
- ▲ To make the filling, start with heating olive oil in a pan.
- ▲ To the hot pan add ½ of the onions, and ½ of the garlic and sauté for about 5 minutes.
- ▲ After the onions turn translucent, add in the mushrooms and sauté on medium heat for about 5 minutes.
- ▲ Next, add the cabbage and sauté for 5 more minutes.
- ▲ Sprinkle salt & pepper to taste and 1 tbsp of soy sauce and mix well.
- ▲ After the cabbage and mushrooms shrink down to half their size, your filling is ready.
- ▲ After the wonton filling is ready, start working on the Thai Curry soup.
- ▲ In a pot add olive oil, and once the oil is hot add the remaining ½ of the onions & garlic.
- ▲ Sauté on medium-low heat for about 5 minutes.
- ▲ Then add 2 heaping tablespoons of red Thai curry paste, and sauté.
- ▲ Add 1 cup of vegetable stalk, and wait for it to come to a boil, then add 1 tbsp of fish sauce and 1 tbsp of soy sauce and stir.
- ▲ Then add 2 cups of coconut milk and stir until it comes to a boil. Add salt to taste.

- Let the soup simmer for about 10 minutes, then taste to adjust the seasoning and finish cooking the soup with a squeeze of lemon juice.
- Now, get back to your dough. Roll the dough and cut it into square pieces – these are your wonton wrappers.
- Add 1 tsp of the mushroom filling in each of the square pieces.
- To make the wonton shape, take one corner of the square wrapper and fold it over the filling to meet the opposite corner, forming a triangle. Press the edges together, making sure there is no air trapped inside and the edges are sealed tightly.
- Once all the wontons are formed, boil them in salted water till nearly translucent. This will take a maximum of 5 minutes.
- To assemble the dish, in a bowl place your desired number of cooked wontons, add a ladle-full of the red Thai Curry soup, and top with a drizzle of chili oil.

Top Tips:

- This recipe is perhaps the most time-consuming out of all the recipes in this book. However, you can make the wontons ahead of time and boil them when you are ready to eat.
- To reduce the time, you can use any gluten-free frozen dumplings and only prepare the soup yourself.
- This dish is naturally vegetarian, and relished by everyone!
- To make the dish look prettier, you can top it with the green part of finely chopped green onions.
- If you enjoy Asian food, you will definitely want to make this recipe again and again!

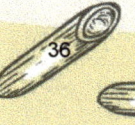

Garlic–Butter Shrimp

Ingredients:
1. 500 grams of peeled and deveined shrimp
2. Extra virgin olive oil
3. Red chili powder
4. Salt
5. Chili Oil
6. Lemon
7. Butter
8. 5 garlic cloves, minced

Method:
- To marinate the shrimp, add 4 tbsps of olive oil, ½ tsp of red chili powder, salt to taste, 1 tsp of chili oil, and the juice of half a lemon.
- Marinate the shrimp at least 30 minutes before cooking.
- Heat a frying pan and grease with olive oil
- To the hot pan, add the marinated shrimp and cook each side for about 3-4 minutes on high heat.
- Take the cooked shrimp out of the pan and set it aside.
- Turn the heat down to low and add 2 tbsps of butter.
- As the butter melts, add the minced garlic and sauté for about 2 minutes.

- ▲ As the garlic becomes aromatic, add the shrimp back in and sauté.
- ▲ Taste and adjust the salt level to your liking.
- ▲ Serve hot!

Top Tips:

- ▲ Ensure you do not overcook the shrimp, to avoid a rubbery texture.
- ▲ Use butter generously, after all, butter makes the body of this dish.
- ▲ This garlic butter shrimp is best served over rice or with pasta.
- ▲ This recipe comes together in a matter of a few minutes, and tastes fantastic!

Egg Fried Rice

Ingredients:
1. A cup of rice
2. Green onions - chopped with the white part and green part separated
3. 2 cloves of garlic, minced
4. 1 egg
5. Soy sauce
6. White vinegar
7. Salt
8. Pepper
9. Chili oil
10. Vegetable oil
11. Sesame oil

Method:
- In a deep frying pan, or wok, heat vegetable oil.
- When the pan is hot, add the white part of the green onion and sauté on high heat for about 3 minutes.
- As the onion turns translucent, add the garlic and sauté for another minute.
- Crack the egg in a bowl, and season with salt and pepper and whisk.
- Then add the egg and scramble in the pan/wok.

- ▲ Once the egg is cooked, add the rice.
- ▲ Break apart the rice and sauté for 3 minutes.
- ▲ Season with salt to taste, 1 tbsp of soy sauce, 1 tsp of white vinegar, 1 tbsp of sesame oil and cook the rice for about 6-7 minutes.
- ▲ Sprinkle the green part of the chopped green onion.
- ▲ Serve the fried rice hot, with a drizzle of chili oil on top.

Top Tips:

- ▲ If you own a wok, use it, it makes all the difference.
- ▲ Use 1 day old rice, rather than freshly cooked rice, it makes the fried rice taste a lot better.
- ▲ Feel free to add another protein like chicken or shrimp or some more vegetables.
- ▲ Keep tasting the seasoning as you go.
- ▲ This recipe is quick and easy, without compromising on the taste.
- ▲ This recipe is naturally gluten-free!

Shrimp Tacos

Ingredients:

1. 500g peeled and deveined shrimp
2. Red chili powder
3. Salt
4. Chili oil
5. Lemon
6. Olive oil
7. Corn tortillas
8. Mayonnaise
9. Lettuce

Method:

- To marinate the shrimp - add 4 tbss of olive oil, ½ tsp of red chili powder, salt to taste, 1 tsp of chili oil, and the juice of half a lemon.
- Marinate the shrimp for at least 30 minutes before cooking.
- In a pan, heat olive oil, and add the shrimp.
- Cook the shrimp on each side for 4-5 minutes on high heat.
- When done, take the shrimp out of the pan and set it aside.
- To prepare the dressing, in a small bowl, add in 4 tsp of mayonnaise, 1 tsp of chili oil, 1 tsp olive oil, salt to taste, and the juice of half a lemon and whisk.
- In a separate flat-top pan, warm up a corn tortilla.

▲ To assemble the soft shell tacos, place a warm tortilla on a plate, layer it with lettuce leaves, then place a few pieces of shrimp and add the dressing on top. Serve warm!

Top Tips:

▲ Ensure you don't overcook the shrimp, to avoid a rubbery texture.

▲ This recipe is quick and easy to prepare and makes for a great lunch or dinner idea.

▲ You can add any toppings of your liking to the tacos, such as tomatoes, guacamole, sour cream, etc.

▲ Ensure that you check the ingredients list on the package of the corn tortillas to double-check if it is gluten-free or not.

Caramelized Onion Pasta

Ingredients:
1. Extra virgin olive oil
2. 1 onion, sliced finely length-wise (in a half-moon shape)
3. 4 garlic cloves, minced
4. Sundried tomatoes, chopped into small pieces
5. 250ml cream
6. ½ cup grated parmesan cheese
7. Salt
8. Pepper
9. Oregano
10. Chili Oil
11. Rice pasta/Lentil pasta

Method:
- In a hot pan, drizzle a generous amount of extra virgin olive oil.
- Then, add the sliced onions to the pan, and immediately sprinkle in some salt, sauté the onions for about 10 minutes on medium-low heat, or until beautifully browned (caramelized).
- Whilst the onions are cooking, in a different pot, heat water, salt it and start boiling your rice/lentil pasta. Cook the pasta as per package instructions.
- To the caramelized onions, add in the garlic and sauté for another minute.

- Then, add the chopped sundried tomatoes, along with some of the oil from the jar of sundried tomatoes, and sauté for 2 minutes.
- Next, add 250 ml of cream and wait for it to reach a simmer.
- When the sauce starts simmering, add salt, pepper, and oregano to taste.
- Then, add the pasta, and mix, until well combined.
- Taste and adjust the seasoning.
- Next, turn off the heat and add the parmesan cheese, along with one ladle of pasta water.
- Stir the pasta until the cheese melts in.
- Serve the pasta hot in a bowl, and optimally top with chili oil.

Top Tips:

- Ensure you give the onions enough time to caramelize, they are the star of this dish.
- Cook the pasta for 2 minutes less than what is instructed on the package, because the pasta will finish cooking in the sauce. This will avoid overcooked pasta.
- This pasta dish is creamy and comforting and comes together very easily!

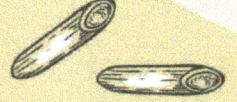
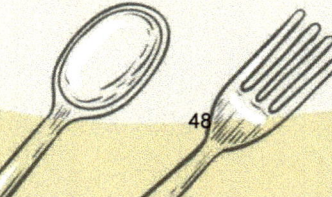

Chocolate Cupcakes

Ingredients:

1. 3/4 cup hot water
2. 1/3 cup melted milk chocolate chips
3. 1 tsp instant coffee powder
4. 1/3 cup Dutch cocoa powder
5. 3/4 cup gluten-free all-purpose flour blend
6. 3/4 cup powdered sugar
7. 1/4 tsp salt
8. 1/2 tsp baking soda
9. 1/3 cup olive oil
10. 2 large eggs
11. 1 tsp white vinegar
12. 2 tsp vanilla essence

Method:

- Preheat your oven to 175°C.
- Prepare the mini-cupcake tray by placing cupcake liners in the tray ahead of time.
- Melt the chocolate chips in the microwave, in 30-second intervals, mixing between each interval until fully melted.
- Add 3/4 cup of hot water into a large mixing bowl.

- Carefully pour in the melted chocolate chips, instant coffee powder, and cocoa powder.
- Whisk well together until the ingredients have fully combined.
- Add the dry ingredients (gluten-free flour, powdered sugar, salt, and baking soda) into the wet ingredients (chocolate and coffee mixture), and mix well until fully blended.
- Crack in the eggs, add the olive oil, vinegar, and vanilla essence, and mix well until a smooth batter is formed.
- Let the batter sit for about 30 minutes to an hour. **(Optional)**
- Fill the prepared cupcake liners 3/4 of the way full, and bake for about 15-20 minutes.
- Allow the cupcakes to cool completely before frosting, adding any toppings or serving.
- Top the cupcakes with Nutella, or your favorite chocolate/vanilla frosting. **(Optional)**
- Decorate with sprinkles or mini chocolate chips. **(Optional)**

Top Tips:

- Overmix your batter - this is usually looked down upon in regular baking, but in gluten-free baking, it is a game-changer. Overmixing the batter allows for your cupcakes to be fluffier while baking.
- Measure vanilla essence with your heart.
- Use the best quality cocoa powder you can find; Dutch cocoa powder usually works well.

▲ Ensure the gluten-free flour that you use is suitable for baking, and has 'Xanthan Gum' listed as one of the ingredients.

▲ Ensure the eggs are at room temperature before using them.

▲ Do not skip the coffee, it really helps awaken the rich chocolate flavor.

▲ Let the batter rest for about 30 minutes to an hour before baking.

▲ This recipe can also be used to make the spongiest cake, if you are not a fan of cupcakes.

Rice Cake Delights

Ingredients:
1. Rice cakes
2. Peanut butter
3. Melted chocolate chips
4. Thinly sliced strawberries
5. Flaky sea salt

Method:
- On top of the rice cakes, spread a tablespoon of peanut butter using a knife.
- For the next layer, spoon on melted chocolate and spread, ensuring that it does not combine with the peanut butter.
- Wait for about 5 minutes for the melted chocolate to harden OR put it in the freezer to speed up the process.
- Then, on top of the chocolate layer, place a few thinly sliced strawberries in a circular pattern using the edges of the rice cake as a guide.
- Lastly, sprinkle on some flaky sea salt.
- Serve immediately, or keep refrigerated to enjoy later!

Top Tips:

- ▲ This recipe takes about 10 minutes to come together and is the easiest way to satiate that craving for dessert.

- ▲ You can use toasted nuts, or any other fruits & berries as toppings.

- ▲ You can use any nut butter instead of peanut butter like almond butter, if you prefer it.

- ▲ This can also make for a good quick snack or an easy sweet breakfast.

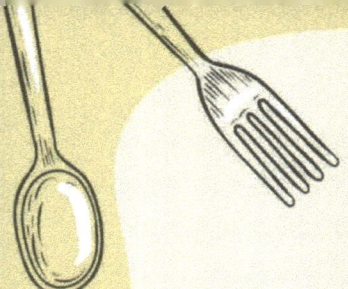

Brownies

Ingredients:

1. 150 g milk chocolate
2. ½ cup unsalted butter
3. 1 cup powdered sugar
4. ½ cup packed brown sugar
5. 3 medium size eggs
6. ¼ tsp salt
7. 2 tsp vanilla essence
8. ½ cup gluten-free all-purpose flour
9. ¼ cup cocoa powder

Method:

- First, preheat your oven to 180 degrees Celsius
- Using a sharp knife, chop the chocolate into small pieces.
- Add the chopped chocolate in a microwave-safe bowl, along with the butter. Place the bowl in the microwave and melt the chocolate and butter together. Between every 30 seconds, take the chocolate out of the microwave and stir using a spoon. Repeat this process till the butter and chocolate are fully melted and well combined. Then set this mixture aside.

- ▲ In a separate large mixing bowl, add the powdered sugar and the brown sugar and whisk them together.
- ▲ Next, add in one egg to the above, and beat using an electric mixer for 4 minutes.
- ▲ Repeat this process for the other 2 eggs.
- ▲ Then pour in the vanilla extract, sprinkle in salt and mix.
- ▲ Then, to the whipped eggs & sugar, add the melted butter and chocolate that had been set aside in the beginning.
- ▲ Add the dry ingredients, that is, the gluten-free all-purpose flour and the cocoa powder, and fold it into the wet ingredients using a rubber spatula.
- ▲ The brownie batter is done here!
- ▲ Line a square baking pan with parchment paper, and grease with butter.
- ▲ Pour the brownie batter into the pan, and tap the pan on the counter-top to ensure the batter is well spread-out.
- ▲ Bake the preheated oven for 20 minutes.
- ▲ Once the brownies are done, a fork should come out clean, when poked into the baked brownies.
- ▲ Cool the brownies for 30 minutes before slicing and serving!

Top Tips:

- ▲ Ensure the eggs are at room temperature before using them.
- ▲ It is crucial that you whip the eggs and sugar well, to get a crinkly crust on top of the brownies.
- ▲ Every oven is different, so the bake time may vary, so keep checking on the brownie every 5 minutes after the 15-minute mark.

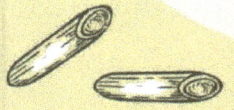

- These brownies are best enjoyed with a scoop of vanilla ice cream.
- These are the best gluten-free brownies that you will ever eat, and the batter comes together pretty quickly!

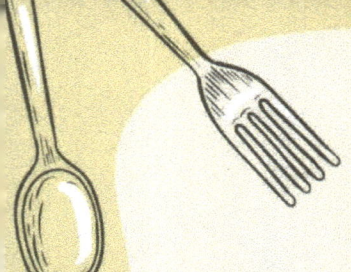

Blondies

Ingredients:
1. 2 eggs
2. 2 tsp vanilla essence
3. 1 cup packed brown sugar
4. ½ cup unsalted butter, melted
5. 1 and ½ cup gluten-free all-purpose flour
6. 1 tsp baking powder
7. ¼ tsp salt
8. 1 cup milk/dark chocolate chips

Method:
- Firstly, preheat the oven to 180 degrees Celsius.
- In a large mixing bowl, crack in 2 eggs.
- In the bowl, add in the vanilla essence, and the packed brown sugar, and whisk until well combined.
- Then, add the melted unsalted butter, and whisk immediately.
- Next, add the gluten-free all-purpose flour, baking powder, and salt, and whisk until the dry ingredients are fully incorporated into the wet ingredients.
- The best part is next; add in the chocolate chips, and fold them into the batter using a rubber spatula.

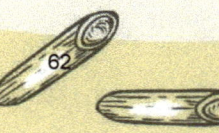

- Line a square baking pan with parchment paper, and grease with butter.
- Pour in the blondie batter in the pan and ensure that the batter is well spread and there is an even layer on top.
- Bake the blondies in the preheated oven for 15-20 minutes.
- Once the blondies are done, a fork should come out clean, when poked into the baked blondies.

Top Tips:

- This recipe is extremely simple, so if you are a beginner, you could start baking with this.
- Ensure the eggs are at room temperature before using them.
- Every oven is different, and the bake time may vary, so keep checking on the brownie every 5 minutes after the 10-minute mark.
- This recipe is the perfect cross-section between a chocolate-chip cookie and a brownie - because it has the flavor profile of a chocolate chip cookie and the texture of a brownie.
- It is recommended that you use the best quality chocolate chips available because that makes all the difference in this recipe.

Roti Revival is a celebration of gluten-free cooking. Roti nourishes warm and whole but a gluten-free menu can also feed the soul. Having navigated gluten intolerance throughout my adolescence, these recipes hold a special place in my heart. While my intolerance has faded, my passion for gluten-free cooking remains strong. This book, the result of four years of dedicated work, features 18 recipes—either naturally gluten-free or adapted with gluten-free ingredients. From teens to adults, whether you're managing dietary restrictions or simply exploring, this collection welcomes you to discover flavorful, wholesome meals that promote health and inclusivity for all.

Thank you for joining me on this gluten-free culinary adventure! Each recipe in this book reflects my journey of discovery, creativity, and the joy of sharing meals with loved ones. Cooking is a beautiful way to connect, and I hope these dishes inspire you to experiment and savour every bite. Happy cooking!

www.ingramcontent.com/pod-product-compliance
Lightning Source LLC
LaVergne TN
LVHW061631070526
838199LV00071B/6644